D1535402

THE MESSIANIC PASSOVER HAGGADAH

MICHAEL LAMBERT

THE MESSIANIC PASSOVER HAGGADAH

MICHAEL LAMBERT

The Messianic Passover Haggadah
Copyright © 2015 by Michael Lambert

Published by Reality Creations Publishing
P.O. Box 472582
Garland, TX 75047
www.realitycreationspublishing.com

All rights reserved. No part of this book may be reproduced or transmitted in any form or by any means, electronic or mechanical, including photocopying and recording without permission in writing from the publisher. The only exception is brief quotations for review purposes.

Unless otherwise indicated, all Scripture quotations are taken from The Holy Bible, New King James Version®, Copyright © 1982 by Thomas Nelson, Inc. Used by permission. All rights reserved.

ISBN-13: 978-0-9964211-2-6

ISBN-10: 0996421122

Cover Design by Bethany Stephens
Senior Editor, Bunni Pounds
Editing and Interior Design by J. Nicole Williamson
www.kingslantern.com

Printed in the United States of America

CONTENTS

PART ONE

INTRODUCING PASSOVER

In ancient Israel, there were three great yearly feasts held in Jerusalem to which every man was to come and observe. Pesach (Passover) was the first, and Shavuot (the Feast of Weeks also called Pentecost) was next — Sheva being the Hebrew word for seven (there are 7 seven-day periods [7 weeks] from Passover to Shavuot or Pentecost — pente means five; Pentecost is the fiftieth day from Passover). The third major feast was in the fall called Sukkot (also Tabernacles or the Feast of Tabernacles).

This little book is called a Haggadah. The word Haggadah means: "the telling." It is the telling of the story of Pesach or Passover. There are many Jewish Haggadahs and Messianic Haggadahs. This Haggadah is intended to be a short service with all the basics and some explanations as to the telling of Passover.

Each generation of Jews should consider themselves as having been personally delivered from Egypt, just as each believer should consider themselves as having been personally delivered from the world. Redemption and cleansing from sin is a personal experience for each person to celebrate.

The central theme of Passover is the miraculous coming out of bondage and into freedom through the blood of the Lamb.

Just as a spotless lamb is slain in the Exodus Passover story, so Jesus, Son of God and Messiah of Israel, is slain on Pesach (Matt. 16:13-17). However, He is resurrected and walks the earth for forty days and is received into heaven. On Pentecost (the fiftieth day), He pours out His Spirit (Acts 2).

What we now celebrate as communion or the Lord's Supper had its origin in the Passover Supper. Jesus said, in Luke 22, "Now the Feast of Unleavened Bread drew near, which is Passover.... Then came the Day of Unleavened Bread, when the Passover must be killed. And He sent Peter and John saying, 'Go and prepare the Passover for us that we may eat.'... So they went and found it just as He had said to them, and they prepared the Passover. When the hour had come, He sat down and the twelve apostles with Him. Then He said to them, 'With fervent desire I have desired to eat this Passover with you before I suffer; for I say to you, I will no longer eat of it until it is fulfilled in the kingdom of God.' Then He took the cup and gave thanks, and said, 'Take this and divide it among yourselves; for I say to you I will not drink of the fruit of the vine until the kingdom of God comes.'

And He took bread, gave thanks and broke it, and gave it to them, saying, 'This is My body which is given for you, do this in remembrance of Me.'

Likewise He also took the cup after supper saying, 'This cup is the new covenant in My blood which is shed for you.'" (Luke 22:1, 7-8,13-20)

In Exodus 12:14, God says of Passover, "This day will become a memorial for you, and you will celebrate it as a festival to the Lord – you will celebrate it perpetually as a lasting ordinance." (NET)

Through this Haggadah, we honor the memorial of Passover by keeping the feast of the Lord — we retell the story of the Lamb for our deliverance.

THE PASSOVER CELEBRATION BEGINS

BLOWING THE SHOFAR

Traditionally, a shofar is blown at the start of the New Year on Rosh Hashanah. A commandment was given in the law (Torah) that on the first day of the seventh month (Tishrei) "...you shall have a sabbath-*rest,* a memorial of blowing of trumpets, a holy convocation." (Lev. 23:24b).

A shofar is an instrument of breath. When God breathed the life of His Spirit into them on Pentecost, there were one hundred and twenty human instruments that He breathed on and who gave out the cry of the Spirit, speaking in other tongues and giving praise to God.

We blow the shofar tonight to celebrate our freedom. It is a ram's horn, blown by musicians in the temple, blown in celebration and blown by warriors in battle. We are all of these three expressions tonight.

LIGHTING THE CANDLES

As we kindle the lights, we pray for the illumination of the Spirit of God to bring personal meaning to the Passover. We remember our passage from Egypt into freedom and redemption.

A woman (lighting the candles) says:

BA-RUCH A-TAH ADO-NOI ELO-HEI-NU HA-OLAM A-SHER KID-SHA-NU BE-MITZ-VO-SAV VE-TZI-VO-NU LE-HAD-LIK NER SHEL YOM TOV

Translation: Blessed are You, Lord our God, King of the Universe, who has sanctified us with His commandments, and has commanded us to kindle the light of the festival day.

We remember that Yeshua (Jesus) is the Light of the world and commanded us to be lights.

Leader

As the candle is kindled by the hand of the woman, we remember that the promised seed of a woman would be the light of the world (Gen. 3:15).

THE FOUR CUPS OF WINE

Leader

We have four cups of wine set before us tonight. Each cup represents a special area of God's redemptive plan for our lives. It is commonly said, the Old Covenant is the New Covenant concealed and the New Covenant is the Old Covenant revealed.

As God spoke to His servant Moses, He revealed His plan for the redemption of the nation of Israel. He then spoke to Yeshua the completion of that plan which included the redemption of the world.

The four cups represent the four "I wills" of God Himself. He will do it.

Everyone

1. I will bring you out from under the yoke of the Egyptians.

2. I will free you from being slaves.

3. I will redeem you with a strong hand and an outstretched arm.

4. I will take you as My own people and I will be your God.

The First Cup

Leader

The first cup is the cup of sanctification. God said, "I will bring you out from under the yoke of the Egyptians."

Let us lift the first cup together and bless the name of the Lord Yeshua.

BA-RUCH A-TAH ADO-NOI ELO-HEI-NU MEL-EK HA-O-LAM BO-REH PE-RI HA-GA-FEN.

Blessed are You, O Lord our God, King of the Universe who creates the fruit of vine.

Let us all drink the cup of sanctification.

THE SEDER PLATE

Leader

Upon our table is the seder plate for the ceremonial meal. At the top are several items: a roasted egg, parsley, lamb shank bone or chicken leg, chopped apples and nuts, horseradish, and bitter herbs. In the middle of our table is salt water.

During the seder we don't just tell and explain the story of the Exodus, we see, we smell, we feel, and we taste the freedom from bondage. We experience the love of God in these elements. As we continue, I will explain what each food is for.

THE WASHING OF HANDS

URKHATZ (Hebrew)

"Who may ascend the hill of the Lord? Who may stand in His Holy Place? He who has clean hands and a pure heart." (Psalms 24:3,4)

Leader

Let us now wash our hands in the bowl of water. On the night of Passover, Yeshua "...poured water into a basin and began to wash the disciples' feet, drying them with a towel that was wrapped around Him... 'Do you understand what I have done for you?' He asked them. 'You call Me Teacher and Lord, and rightly so, for that is what I am. Now that I, your Lord and Teacher, have washed your feet, you also should wash one another's feet.'" (John 13:5, 12-14 NIV)

THE SECOND CUP

THE CUP OF PLAGUES &
THE CUP OF INSTRUCTION

Leader

Moses went to the house of Pharaoh to demand —
Let My people go.

Everyone

"But I know that the king of Egypt will not let you go
unless a mighty hand compels him. So I will stretch
out My hand and strike the Egyptians with all the
wonders that I will perform among them. After that
He will let you go." (Exodus 3:19-20 NIV)

Leader

So God sent plagues and each time Pharaoh
hardened his heart. When God sent the tenth plague
with the death of the firstborn son, Pharaoh let his
people go.

So as we fill the cup a second time, we know this is
also a cup of joy. God gives us deliverance from
Satan and his demons by the death of Yeshua the
Messiah and the shedding of His blood.

Everyone

As we remember the plagues together, let us dip our finger into the cup and allow a drop to fall on the plate — ten drops for the ten plagues.

Together we say passionately: 1. Blood 2. Frogs 3. Lice 4. Beasts 5. Diseased cattle 6. Boils 7. Hail 8. Locusts 9. Darkness 10. Death of the firstborn.

Our freedom came at a price. With a mighty hand and an outstretched arm, Yeshua died on the cross for us.

Blessed is He who keeps His promise to us.

Let us drink together.

THAT WOULD HAVE BEEN ENOUGH

Leader — If He had rescued us from Egypt but not punished the Egyptians

Everyone — DAYENU *that would have been enough*

Leader — If He had punished the Egyptians but not destroyed their gods

Everyone — DAYENU *that would have been enough*

Leader — If He had destroyed their gods but not killed their firstborn

Everyone — DAYENU *that would have been enough*

Leader — If He had killed their firstborn but not given us their property

Everyone — DAYENU *that would have been enough*

Leader — If He had given us their property but not divided the Red Sea before us

Everyone — DAYENU *that would have been enough*

Leader — If He had divided the Red Sea for us but not drowned our oppressors

Everyone — DAYENU *that would have been enough*

Leader — If He had drowned our oppressors but not supplied us in the desert for forty years

Everyone — DAYENU *that would have been enough*

Leader — If He had supplied us in the desert for forty years but not fed us manna

Everyone — DAYENU *that would have been enough*

Leader — If He had fed us with manna but not given us the Sabbath

Everyone — DAYENU *that would have been enough*

Leader — If He had given us Sabbath but not brought us to Mount Sinai

Everyone — DAYENU *that would have been enough*

Leader — If He had brought us to Mount Sinai but not given us the Torah

Everyone — DAYENU *that would have been enough*

Leader — If He had given us Torah but not brought us to the land of promise

Everyone — DAYENU *that would have been enough*

Leader — If He had brought us to the land of promise but not built us the temple

Everyone — DAYENU *that would have been enough*

Leader — If He had built the temple but not provided us permanent salvation

Everyone — DAYENU *that would have been enough*

Leader — But praise the Lord! God provided permanent salvation through the sacrifice of Yeshua the Messiah

Everyone – DAYENU! It was enough. It was enough. It was enough. Hallelujah!

THE FOUR QUESTIONS

Ma Nistanah: "When your children ask you, 'What does this ceremony mean to you?' Then tell them." (Exodus 12:26 NIV)

Young Child

How is this night different from all other nights?

1. On all other nights we eat bread or matzah.

    Why on this night do we only eat matzah?

2. On all other nights we eat all kinds of vegetables.

    Why on this night do we eat only bitter herbs?

3. On all other nights we do not dip our vegetables even once.

    Why on this night do we dip them twice?

4. On all other nights we eat our meals sitting or reclining.

    Why on this night do we eat only reclining?

WE ANSWER THE QUESTIONS

Leader

It is a duty and a privilege to answer the four questions of Passover and recite the mighty works of God.

QUESTION ONE

THE MATZAH — UNLEAVENED BREAD

THE BREAD OF AFFLICTION

Leader

Why on this night do we only eat matzah?

As the children of Israel fled from Egypt, they did not have time to put the leaven in the bread and let the dough rise but instead they baked it flat. Leaven is a symbol of sin.

Everyone

1 Corinthians 5:6-8, "Your glorying is not good. Do you not know that a little leaven leavens the whole lump? Therefore purge out the old leaven, that you may be a new lump, since you truly are unleavened. For indeed Christ, our Passover, was sacrificed for us. Therefore let us keep the feast, not with old leaven, nor with the leaven of malice and wickedness, but with the unleavened *bread* of sincerity and truth."

Leader

(Lifting the plate which contains the three matzah)

The three matzot together are seen by the Rabbis as a "unity." Some see Abraham, Isaac and Jacob in this unity. We who know Messiah see the unity as the Father, Son, and Holy Spirit. In the matzah, we see clearly the picture of Yeshua the Messiah for it is striped, bruised, and pierced.

Everyone

"But He was wounded for our transgressions, He was bruised for our iniquities: the chastisement of our peace was upon Him: and by His stripes we are healed." (Isaiah 53:5)

Leader (holds up the matzah)

See how the matzah is striped and pierced.

Everyone

"And I will pour upon the house of David, and upon the inhabitants of Jerusalem, the Spirit of grace and supplications; and they shall look upon Me whom they have pierced, and they shall mourn for Him as one mourns for His only son..." (Zechariah 12:10 KJV)

Leader (Removes the middle matzah and breaks it)

As Yeshua the Messiah was broken, so is the bread of affliction broken. One half of this is now called the *Afikomen* (He who is coming). It is wrapped in a white cloth just as Messiah's body was wrapped for burial.

(The Leader now wraps the Afikomen and hides it somewhere in the room as the children cover their eyes.)

Leader (Breaks the other piece and asks others to break their pieces, too, and pass them to each other).

BA-RUCH A-TAH ADO-NOI ELO-HEI-NU MEL-EK HA-O-LAM HA-MOTZI LEK-HEM MIN HA-ARETZ.

Everyone

Blessed are You, O Lord, King of the Universe, who brings forth bread from the earth.

QUESTION TWO

THE MAROR — THE BITTER HERBS
AND HORSERADISH

Leader

Why on this night do we eat only bitter herbs?

On all other nights we eat all kinds of vegetables, but on Passover we only eat bitter herbs. Though life is sweet in Yeshua the Messiah, it was bitter for the children of Israel in Egypt and it was bitter for us in a world of sin.

Horseradish

Take a piece of matzah and dip it into the horseradish. The bitter taste reminds us of the years of sorrow in Egypt.

Leader (Recite)

BA-RUCH A-TAH ADO-NOI ELO-HEI-NU MEL-EK
HA-O-LAM ASHER KIDSHANU

B'MITZVOTAV V'TZIVANU AL ACHEELAT MAROR

27

Everyone (Lifting up the matzah with the maror)

Blessed are You, O Lord, King of the Universe, who has set us apart by His Word and commanded us to eat bitter herbs.

QUESTION THREE

THE KHAROSET — WE DIP TWICE THE PARSLEY IN SALT WATER

Leader

Why on this night do we dip them twice?

On all other nights we do not dip our vegetables even once, but tonight we dip them twice.

(Leader dips the parsley into the salt water twice)

The kharoset — brown apple mixture:

The children of Israel worked hard making bricks and clay for the Egyptians. We see this brown mixture made from apples, honey and nuts as the mixture between the bricks holding everything together.

Everyone (Take the bitter herbs — the parsley dipped in saltwater — and dip the parsley into the kharoset and put it on the matzah.)

We dip the bitter herbs into the kharoset remembering that in the most bitter of circumstances, life can be sweet by the love relationship we have with Yeshua.

(Now eat them together)

QUESTION FOUR

Leader

Why tonight do we eat only reclining?

The first Passover was celebrated by a people who were slaves. They were instructed to eat the Passover in a hurry — with loins girded, sandals on their feet, and staffs in their hands — anticipating a quick leave from Egypt.

Tonight, we may all recline and freely enjoy the Passover Seder with rest in Yeshua.

Everyone

Yeshua the Messiah said:

"Come to Me, all you who are weary and heavy laden, and I will give you rest." (Matthew 11:28)

Once we were slaves to sin, but now we are free.

(Here there could be a dancer to a freedom song or just a congregational song of praise.)

THE PASSOVER LAMB

The Hebrew word for
"Passover" is Pesach

"The blood will be a sign for you on the houses
where you are: and when I see the blood, I will pass
over you." (Exodus 12:13a NIV)

Leader

Rabbi Gamaliel, a teacher of Rabbi Saul (Paul the Apostle), taught that in recounting the Passover story a person must mention three things:

1. The unleavened bread – the matzah
2. The bitter herbs – the maror
3. The Passover Lamb – the Pesach

Everyone

We have eaten the matzah that reminds us of the haste when the children of Israel left Egypt. We have tasted the bitter herbs that remind us of their bitter slavery they experienced in Egypt, and of our bitter slavery that we experienced in the world.

Leader

(Lifting the shank bone of the lamb)

This roasted shank bone represents the lamb whose blood marked the houses of the children of Israel. The lamb's blood was put on the doorposts of each house in response to God's command to place it there. It also reminds us of the blood of Yeshua the Messiah, God's Lamb, who shed His blood for each of us. We are marked in that invisible realm with the blood of Christ on our foreheads.

Everyone

We are reminded by Moses that it was the Lord Himself who redeemed Israel from slavery. "So the LORD brought us out of Egypt with a mighty hand and with an outstretched arm, with great terror and with signs and wonders." (Deuteronomy 26:8)

Leader

The temple no longer stands in Jerusalem, but we expect one to be rebuilt. The shank bone remains to remind us of the sacrificial Lamb.

(Lifting the egg)

The egg was later added to the seder and was called khagigah — meaning a special holiday offering. It is a sign of mourning on one hand, yet considered by many to denote new birth and eternal life as its shape has no beginning and no end.

It may be eaten *during* the seder meal.

Everyone

We who have trusted our lives into the hands of Yeshua the Messiah know that He is the Lamb of God, our Passover. Through the shedding of His blood, the second death passes over us. Like the ancient Israelites, we know that it was God Himself and not an angel, it was God Himself and not a seraph, it was God Himself and not a messenger, who delivered us.

———

Yeshua achieved our final redemption from sin and death, through His blood, and has brought us out of the world and into the kingdom of God.

Blessed are You, oh Lord, for You have given us forgiveness of sin, abundant life, life everlasting, and You have provided for every need.

Leader

As we again take the second cup in our hand, we remember what Psalm 145:7 says, "They will celebrate Your abundant goodness and joyfully sing of Your righteousness." (NIV)

So we will sing the song of Moses (Exodus 15:1-2).

I will sing to the Lord,

For He has triumphed gloriously!

The horse and its rider He has thrown into the sea!

The Lord is my strength and song,

And He has become my salvation;

He is my God, and I will praise Him;

My father's God, and I will exalt Him.

Everyone

Blessed are You, oh Lord God, for You have in Your mercy given us Yeshua the Messiah, forgiveness for sin, and life everlasting.

34

THE PASSOVER SUPPER

Shulkhan Oreykah

"You shall keep a feast to the Lord."

Pray over the food in Hebrew or English, or both.

Enjoy the Passover supper!

PART TWO

After Supper

THE AFIKOMEN

The children now hunt for the Afikomen.

When one of the children brings it to the leader, the child is then rewarded with some money.

Leader

This was the hidden bread of the Messiah now revealed — Jesus Himself took the matzah, broke it, and gave thanks to the Lord as He prayed:

BA-RUCH A-TAH ADO-NOI ELO-HEI-NU MEL-EK HA-O-LAM HA-MOTZI LEK-HEM MIN HA-ARETZ.

Everyone

Blessed are You, O Lord, King of the Universe, who brings forth bread from the earth.

Leader

It was then that Yeshua added the words.

"This is My body given for you; do this in remembrance of Me." (Luke 22:19b NIV)

Let us take this matzah.

As we allow the taste to linger in our mouths we recognize that the Jews, for centuries after this event would, as a whole, not recognize Yeshua as the hidden bread.

Since Jerusalem was recaptured in 1967, several hundred thousand Jews across the Earth have had their eyes opened to the fact of Yeshua being the Messiah and Son of God. So it behooves us to continue to pray for their salvation as God Himself is lifting the blindness off His people. Jews are preaching this same gospel in the nation of Israel, even today.

THE THIRD CUP

THE CUP OF REDEMPTION

Leader

Let us fill our cups for the third time.

(Then lifting the cup)

This is the cup of redemption. It was the cup after the supper where Yeshua identifies Himself as the Messiah.

Everyone

"I will redeem you with an outstretched arm." (Exodus 6:6)

"Therefore His own arm brought salvation for Him, and His own righteousness, it sustained Him." (Isaiah 59:16)

Leader

Yeshua the Messiah, Son of God, lifted the cup and said:

"This cup is the new covenant in My blood, which is poured out for you." (Luke 22:20)

Everyone

BA-RUCH A-TAH ADO-NOI ELO-HEI-NU MEL-EK HA-O-LAM BO-REH PE-RI HA-GA-FEN.

___

Blessed are You, O Lord our God, King of the Universe who creates the fruit of vine.

Let us all drink the cup of redemption.

THE PROPHET ELIJAH

ELIJAHU HA HANAVI

Leader

We have sat an extra place at the table. This is the place and the cup of Elijah the Prophet. Elijah did not see death but instead was swept up in a whirlwind. We hoped he would come tonight.

(One of the children goes to a door and opens the door to welcome Elijah to the seder.)

Everyone

"See I will send the prophet Elijah to you before that great and dreadful day of the Lord comes." (Malachi 4:5 NIV)

Leader

Yeshua spoke about John the Baptist.

"And If you are willing to accept it, he is the Elijah who was to come." (Matthew 11:14 NIV)

Perhaps he will come next year.

THE FOURTH CUP

THE CUP OF PRAISE

Leader
Let us fill the fourth and final cup and give thanks to God.

Leader — Give thanks to the Lord, for He is good

Everyone — His mercies endure forever

Leader — Give thanks to the God of gods

Everyone — His mercies endure forever

Leader — Give thanks to the Lord of lords

Everyone — His mercies endure forever

Leader — to Him who alone does great wonders

Everyone — His mercies endure forever

Leader — who by His understanding made the heavens

Everyone — His mercies endure forever

Leader — who spread out the earth upon the waters

Everyone — His mercies endure forever

Leader — who made the great lights

Everyone — His mercies endure forever

Leader — the sun to govern the day

Everyone — His mercies endure forever

Leader — and the moon and stars to govern the night

Everyone — His mercies endure forever

Leader — to Him who struck down the firstborn of Egypt

Everyone — His mercies endure forever

Leader — and brought out Israel out from among them

Everyone — His mercies endure forever

Leader — with a mighty hand and an outstretched arm

Everyone — His mercies endure forever

Leader — to Him who divided the Red Sea asunder

Everyone — His mercies endure forever

Leader — and brought Israel through the midst of it

Everyone — His mercies endure forever

Leader — but swept Pharaoh and his army into the Red Sea

Everyone — His mercies endure forever

Leader — to Him who led His people through the desert

Everyone — His mercies endure forever

Leader — Give thanks to the God of heaven

Everyone — His mercies endure forever

(Psalm 136:1-16, 26 NIV)

Leader (Lifting the cup for the last time)
Let us lift up the cup of praise and bless the name of the Lord.

Everyone

BA-RUCH A-TAH ADO-NOI ELO-HEI-NU MEL-EK HA-O-LAM BO-REH PE-RI HA-GA-FEN.

Blessed are You, O Lord our God, King of the universe who creates the fruit of the vine.

Everyone — His mercies endure forever (3x)

Leader — Our Passover is now complete just as our redemption and deliverance out of the world is complete.

Next year in Jerusalem!

*LASHANAH HABA BA
YERUSHALAYIM*

About the Author

Michael Lambert

After forty years of being involved in Israel, observing and doing Passovers, working as a missionary, teacher, pastor, and prophet, Mike Lambert has written this abbreviated version of the Passover Haggadah.

Mike and his wife, Helen, went to Israel the first time in 1975 as volunteers on a Kibbutz. A few years later they returned and spent nearly fifteen years living and pastoring in Jerusalem while raising their five children in the land.

Mike and Helen have travelled the world teaching at missions, conferences, churches, and Bible Schools. They are the founders of the ministry Jerusalem Descending, and are co-founders and network leaders of Reality Community, a network of house churches.

Mike has a Master's degree of Divinity from King's University, a Bachelor's and Master's degree in Biblical Studies from Logos University, and an Associate's degree of Practical Theology from Christ for the Nations Institute.

Mike and Helen have consistently shared the love of Christ, the message of the restoration of the Church to the gifts and power of the Holy Spirit, as well as the message of a dispersed Jewish people being restored to their land and the reconciliation of the Jewish people to their Messiah, Yeshua, the Son of God.

Even so, come quickly, Lord Jesus

Reality Community: our Church

Whole-hearted believers in Jesus —
united in worship, mission and community.

www.realitycommunitytexas.com

REALITY CREATIONS PUBLISHING was founded to provide resources for our local church, the Body of Christ at large, and to be a blessing to the nations. We pray that each product, whether it is music or books, blesses your life, your ministry, and the people around you.

All of our products are available at special quantity discounts for bulk purchase. This is for the benefit of a local church, as well as to help individuals who want to disciple others in the Word of God or to take these products around the world.

You can book one of our authors to speak at your church or ministry. Mike and Helen are also available to help facilitate a Passover in your area.

For details, go to our website at:
www.realitycreationspublishing.com

Or write us at:
Reality Creations
P.O. Box 472582, Garland, TX 75047

CPSIA information can be obtained
at www.ICGtesting.com
Printed in the USA
LVOW05s1021250717
542446LV00047B/237/P